Real Estate Riches

Build Your Empire Through Property

Table of Contents

Chapter 1. Introduction

Immerse yourself in the lucrative world of real estate with our Special Report, "Real Estate Riches: Build Your Empire Through Property." This meticulously compiled report unveils the most proven and powerful strategies to amass wealth through property investments, offering you a practical guide through the twists and turns of the real estate empire-building journey. Suited to both novices exploring their first venture and seasoned moguls seeking to diversify, this report promises to invigorate your aspirations into tangible action plans. Discover the secrets to successful property acquisitions, gain insights into market trends, and learn the art of risk management, all to unlock the door to your financial freedom. Prepare to take your first step on the path to property prosperity!

Chapter 2. Foundation of Real Estate Investing

Before embarking on the rewarding journey of real estate investing, there are fundamental concepts, principles, and strategies that you need to grasp. Understanding these foundations will equip you with the knowledge and use it as a springboard to launch your empire-building ventures successfully.

2.1. UNDERSTANDING REAL ESTATE AND ITS TYPES

Real estate encapsulates land, along with any permanent improvements attached to it. This includes buildings, homes, fences, and any other fixtures or facilities considered 'immovable'. This market segmentation of real estate furthers into four primary categories:

- **Residential Real Estate:** This category includes properties like single-family homes, townhouses, duplexes, high-value homes, multi-generational, and vacation homes.

- **Commercial Real Estate:** These are income-generating properties used for business purposes, such as shopping centers, hotels, office buildings, and apartment complexes.

- **Industrial Real Estate:** These properties include manufacturing buildings, warehouses, and properties that can be used for research, production, storage, and large-scale distribution of goods.

- **Raw Land Real Estate:** This includes undeveloped, early development or reuse, subdivision, and site assembly plots.

Each type comes with its own set of opportunities, challenges, pros, and cons, which will be elucidated in the following chapters. Understanding your financial landscape, risk tolerance, and market research will help you pinpoint the type of real estate that suits your investment style.

2.2. PRINCIPLES OF REAL ESTATE INVESTMENT

A successful real estate investment journey is based on a firm grasp of several essential principles:

- **Market Research and Analysis:** Understanding market dynamics, future trends, and demographic shifts are crucial in making informed decisions before committing to a property investment.

- **Risk Management:** Pondering the various risks associated with real estate investing and counteracting them with suitable strategies ensures your investment is secure.

- **Investment Diversification:** Distributing your investments across different types of properties can mitigate risks and optimize potential returns.

- **Location is Key:** The location of your property plays a crucial role in determining its future value and investment potential.

- **Patience Pays:** Real estate investing often demands long-term commitment and patience to allow your investment to appreciate.

These principles form the backbone of any successful real estate investment strategy and will be explored at length in the course of this report.

2.3. GETTING STARTED: CREATING YOUR INVESTMENT PLAN

When it comes to real estate, jumping in without a plan is likely to result in failure. This section will guide you through the critical steps to creating a robust, comprehensive investment plan.

- **Assess Your Financial Wellness:** Understanding your current financial position, including your income, expenses, savings, debt, and credit score, is the first step to planning your real estate investment journey.

- **Set Defined Goals:** Your goals should be Specific, Measurable, Attainable, Relevant, and Time-Bound (SMART). A well-defined goal propels your strategy forward with clarity.

- **Budgeting and Financing:** No plan would be complete without a proper understanding of various financing options, budgeting requirements, and calculating potential returns on investment.

- **Building A Real Estate Team:** Surrounding yourself with a knowledgeable, experienced real estate team is an invaluable asset to invest effectively.

- **Property Analysis:** Finally, piece together the information about the property, including its current value, potential growth, estimated renovation costs, and long-term value prediction.

2.4. THE POWER OF LEVERAGING IN REAL ESTATE

Leveraging or using borrowed capital to increase the potential return of an investment is powerful in real estate. This could either act as a catalyst that propels you towards your financial goals or as a destructive force if not handled with caution. Understanding the proper use of leverage, mitigating its associated risks, and aligning it to fit your investment strategy is a must - knowledge of which will be provided within this report.

2.5. REAL ESTATE LEGAL ASPECTS

Lastly, every real estate investor ought to be familiar with the legal aspects that govern property ownership, transfer, leasing, tax, and more. These laws vary by country and state, making it essential for you to comprehend the laws that apply to your area of investment.

In conclusion, understanding the robust foundations of real estate investing is instrumental to success. With these foundational concepts and principles in hand, you will navigate complexities, seize opportunities, mitigate risks, and drive your journey towards building a prosperous real estate empire.

Chapter 3. Understanding Different Property Types

Just as matters of 'location, location, location' rule supreme in the property market, it is equally significant to understand the different types of assets available in the spectrum. The deeper the knowledge you have about the varieties, the better informed will be your investment decisions and the higher your chances of striking gold.

3.1. Residential Properties

The most prevalent and diverse category, residential properties comprise single-family homes, apartments, condominiums, townhouses, duplexes, and even mobile homes. Although these types are quite varied in themselves, the fundamental leitmotif remains the same - to provide accommodation to people.

While investing in these properties, consider their capacity for rent, appreciation, and the rate of vacancy. This will provide an accurate estimation of the potential return on investment (ROI). You'll also need to account for the maintenance costs, property taxes, and transaction fees.

Single-family homes can be advantageous due to their wide renter base and simple management regulations. Conversely, apartments and multi-family residential properties allow property owners to acquire multiple rents together.

3.2. Commercial Properties

These comprise office buildings, retail spaces, warehouses, and specialty markets like car washes, self-storage, and bowling alleys. Commercial real estate investments are often more complex as they typically involve multi-year leases and may require higher initial investments. However, they can be quite lucrative for the receptive investor who understands market trends and tenant needs.

Office buildings, the cornerstone of commercial property, can be classified into Class A, B, and C, based on factors like location quality and infrastructure. A prime understanding of these classes can help an investor decide on a niche of focus.

Retail spaces include shopping centers, strip malls, and individual retail stores. Lease agreements in retail often include a base rent plus a percentage of sales revenue, assuring the owner will profit as the tenant's business thrives.

3.3. Industrial Properties

Industrial properties include warehouses, factories, and distribution centers. Industrial real estate caters more to businesses than individual tenants, with long lease durations and generally lower operating costs. These properties often have larger footprints, and the values depend significantly on the location, especially proximity to transport hubs.

Moreover, these warehouses can also be transformed into 'flex' spaces, accommodating offices, distribution centers, and light manufacturing units all under the same roof. This flexibility can increase property value and attract a wider range of tenants.

3.4. Mixed-use Properties

A blend of residential, commercial, and sometimes industrial spaces, mixed-use properties are real estate's answer to the rise in urbanization and changing societal trends. Developers are integrating different property types into one project to provide convenience and opportunities for community building.

Mixed-use properties can be quite complex but have the potential for substantial returns. Not only do they diversify risk across multiple tenants, but they also attract a range of renters, creating a community environment that can help to ensure ongoing profitability and reduced vacancies.

3.5. Raw Land

Investing in undeveloped land can be a high-yield proposition if you are willing to put in the work. Locations near urban areas, or those earmarked for future development, could spell gold for investors. However, it is generally a longer-term play and carries a higher risk as there are no cash flows through rents, and dealing with zoning regulations can be complex.

In real estate, understanding different types of property investments is crucial in defining your investment strategy. By carefully evaluating the advantages and risks associated, you can ensure that your property portfolio gives you the profits you desire. Always remember to factor in market trends and projections when deciding on your investments. As the famous mantra of real estate investing goes, it's all about 'location, location, location'.

Whether you are starting with a small residential property or a large commercial space, the key lies in astutely planning your moves, doing your homework, and understanding the intricacies of the property types you are investing in. Remember, in the end, successful real estate investing is as much about instinct as it's about the financials.

Next, we would transition into Specialty Real Estate and continue to explore the manifold dimensions of different property types.

Chapter 4. Analyzing Market Trends: The Key to Success

The importance of astute and informed analysis of market trends in real estate cannot be understated. This sophisticated understanding acts as a navigational compass in your property investment voyage. It allows you to identify shifts in demand, anticipate market swings, and predict emerging hotspots, all essential to designing lucrative investment strategies. Blending both quantitative and qualitative analyses, this chapter offers a holistic guide to investigating ever-evolving market trends.

4.1. Understanding Market Fundamentals

To analyze real estate market trends effectively, grounding your analysis on strong market fundamentals is essential. These fundamentals consist of a few key factors:

- Population Growth: A growing population indicates a steady demand for housing, which can lead to increased property values and rental income.

- Economic Growth: Regions with robust local economies often see more demand for commercial and residential properties due to job opportunities.

- Interest Rates: Low interest rates can stimulate property investments and increase property values.

4.1.1. Population Growth

Population growth significantly influences housing demand. Tracking census data of areas, understanding demographic shifts, and observing population migration can lead to exciting investment sights. For example, a movement of young professionals into a city could indicate growing demand for apartments and residential properties in urban cores.

4.1.2. Economic Growth

The local economy's health plays a significant role in real estate market trends. Areas with booming industries, low unemployment levels, or plans for future economic expansion often see increased property demand, therefore attracting real estate investors.

4.1.3. Interest Rates

Interest rates can influence a buyer's purchasing power. Lower interest rates allow potential buyers to afford higher-value homes, increasing demand, and consequently, property values. Conversely, high rates have the opposite effect.

4.2. Applying Analytical Tools

Data and trends analysis become more reliable and efficient with the use of analytical tools. These include Market Cycle Analysis, Comparative Market Analysis, and Future Forecasting.

4.2.1. Market Cycle Analysis

Market Cycle Analysis involves studying recurring trends to predict future market behavior. These cycles comprise four phases: Recovery, Expansion, Hyper Supply, and Recession. Predicting the phase your target market is in aids in determining potential investment values.

4.2.2. Comparative Market Analysis

Comparative Market Analysis is a tool to assess a property's market value by comparing it to similar properties sold within a specific period. Property specifics such as location, size, amenities, and condition weigh in the analysis. This tool aids in avoiding overpriced properties or identifying underpriced opportunities.

4.2.3. Future Forecasting

Despite its inherent uncertainties, future forecasting is essential to stay ahead in real estate. It involves identifying emerging trends and potential changes in market fundamentals. Tools such as predictive analytics and market indicators foster reliable forecasts to shape your investment strategies.

4.3. Evaluating Legal and Regulatory Trends

Sometimes, trends in the realm of laws and regulations can dramatically affect the real estate landscape. Changes in zoning laws, construction regulations, tax laws, and environmental laws can affect property values and the desirability of investments. Staying updated with these changes can make a difference in your real estate strategy.

4.4. Assessing Local Trends

While assessing overall market trends is important, understanding micro-trends in specific locations can give you a competitive edge in real estate. Often, the real estate market's temperature can differ significantly from one neighborhood to another. Keep an eye on community development projects, school ratings, crime rates, and forthcoming infrastructure projects to absorb the complete landscape.

4.5. Practicing Risk Management

Establishing a successful real estate portfolio isn't just about identifying profitable investment opportunities; it also involves averting financial mishaps. Regular, comprehensive risk assessment of the market allows investors to insulate their investments against potential downturns.

Analyzing market trends in real estate investment is a delicate blend of art and science. It demands diligent research, continuous learning, and informed decision-making. Arm yourself with this knowledge to make informed predictions and choices, building your success in the dynamic dance of the real estate market. The real estate empire awaits you. Step in with your head held high, and your strategy deeply rooted in understanding market trends.

Chapter 5. Navigating the Intricacies of Property Acquisitions

Entering the world of property acquisitions, you might feel as if you've stepped into a labyrinth. This chapter will guide you through this intricate landscape, revealing the perfect balance between legal obligations, market analysis, negotiation tactics, and timing.

5.1. Identifying the Ideal Property

The first and perhaps the most crucial aspect is identifying the ideal property. The perfect property varies for every investor due to differences in financial circumstances, risk appetite, and investment goals. Create a checklist of what you deem imperative in your ideal property. This approach lends clarity, narrows down search results, and quickens the selection process. Your checklist might include considerations like location, proximity to amenities, potential rental yield, price, and possible capital growth.

A good starting point is to seek properties in areas with excellent potential for appreciation. Market research is paramount at this stage. Identify areas with projected population growth, planned infrastructure developments, and other positive indicators of future property value growth. Utilizing technology, such as online real estate databases and platforms, can play a vital role in identifying the ideal asset.

5.2. Securing Financing

With an ideal property in mind, the next step is to secure financing. Before starting property hunting, speak with a mortgage broker or lender to understand your borrowing power. This pre-approval process not only provides a budget range but also streamlines negotiation and purchase processes once you find your desired property.

Understand all terms, conditions, interest rates, monthly payments, and fees associated with your mortgage. Consider different types of loans such as fixed-rate mortgages, adjustable-rate mortgages, interest-only loans, and negative amortization loans. Each type has its own pros and cons, thus, the decision should be based on your individual circumstances and financial goals.

5.3. Legal Considerations

Acquiring property is not merely a financial transaction, but a legal one too. Understanding the legalese associated with property acquisition can be exhausting, but it's critical for risk management. Hiring a competent real estate attorney can simplify this process. These professionals can scrutinize contacts, sort out title issues and help you navigate through zoning laws.

Understanding all legal obligations, such as transfer duties, stamp duties, and property taxes, is crucial. You should also be aware of any property laws or impending legislation that could impact your purchase; laws related to property use restrictions, landlord and tenant rights, and more.

5.4. The Art of Negotiation

Negotiation can make or break a property deal. The aim is to reach a mutually beneficial agreement, landing a property for a price less than or equal to the amount you had in mind.

Strong negotiation begins with research. Study market trends, property values in the area, and the seller's motivation for selling. An agent can be engaged to conduct these negotiations, primarily if high-stakes or international transactions are involved.

5.5. Closing the Deal

When both parties have reached an agreement, it is time to close the deal. Here, paperwork needs to be finalized. Ensure you review all documents thoroughly before signing them. Your attorney and mortgage lender will guide you in understanding the terms in these documents.

A home inspection is typically the final step before closing. This helps in revealing any flaws or repairs required in the property, providing another chance to negotiate prices or withdraw from the deal if necessary.

Remember, the real estate market uniquely fluctuates. It is influenced by economic factors, government policies, and consumer sentiment. These complications, however, should not deter you from acquiring property. With the right knowledge, the maze of property acquisition becomes a manageable pathway to wealth. Always endeavor to understand the market, exercise due diligence, and most importantly, remain patient and resilient in the face of setbacks. Happy hunting!

Chapter 6. Financing Your Property Investments

Investing in real estate can be a lucrative venture, offering the promise of long-term steady income. However, it's not without its complexities, among which financing is perhaps the most crucial aspect. In this chapter, we demystify the process, provide strategies to leverage, and guide you to make informed financing decisions.

To navigate the waters of property investment, you must be well-versed in the financing options available to you. In doing so, you can compare and contrast, making a decision that aligns your property investment with your financial objectives, risk tolerance, and investment horizon.

6.1. Understanding Mortgages

Mortgages are the most common form of financing for property investments. Essentially, this is a loan you get from a bank or mortgage broker with your property serving as collateral. Should you default, the bank has the right to take ownership of your property and sell it to recoup its investment.

Typically, mortgages would cover up to 80% of your property's value, though this might be higher or lower depending on a range of factors such as your credit score, income stability, and the type of property you're buying.

Understanding the full implications of a mortgage involves more than just interest rates. Other factors to consider include the duration of the mortgage, the type of interest rate (fixed or variable), and other fees involved. Make sure to enlist the help of an experienced attorney to pore over the fine details before signing the dotted lines.

6.2. Exploring Private Financing Options

Private financing is a valuable alternative or supplement to traditional lending methods. This typically involves soliciting funds from friends, family, or professional investors in the form of a loan or equity investment.

Although this route can be complex, often requiring legal and tax advice, it can be quite suitable for those unable to qualify for traditional financing. There are several ways to approach private financing:

1. Personal loans: These can be unsecured (backed only by your promise to repay) or secured (backed by collateral), and can come from anyone willing to lend you money, including friends, family, or private lenders.

2. Equity financing: Wealthy individuals, known as 'angel investors', or institutional investors, may be willing to finance your property in exchange for equity, or a percentage ownership in the property.

3. Seller financing: Here, the property's seller finances your purchase, serving as the lender. This can be a good option if you're unable to secure other forms of financing.

6.3. Real Estate Investment Trusts (REITs)

REITs are companies that own or finance income-producing real estate. By investing in a REIT, you have a stake in their real estate investments. This can be an attractive option if you wish to participate in the real estate market without the need to buy or manage the property yourself.

Investors typically earn through dividends (part of the income the REIT makes from its properties), and any increase in share price. In addition to requiring less capital, REIT investments also provide the added benefit of liquidity, as shares can be bought and sold on the stock market.

6.4. Hard Money Lenders

Hard money lenders offer short-term, high-interest loans based largely on the value of the property being purchased, not on the borrower's credit. This form of financing is often used for 'fix and flip' properties where the buyer plans to quickly resell the property for profit.

While hard money loans involve higher risk and interest rates, they provide quick access to cash, typically without the rigorous approval process of traditional banks. They're a popular choice among investors looking to acquire distressed properties for re-selling.

6.5. Making the Right Choice

When it comes to financing your real estate investment, there's no one-size-fits-all. Each option has its advantages and pitfalls which you must carefully review and match with your financial capability, risk tolerance, and property type. This chapter has equipped you with basic knowledge and understanding of various financing options.

Remember, requesting professional advice can make the difference between a steady income stream and financial distress. An experienced attorney or financial advisor can help you align your choice with your overall investment strategy and long-term goals to ensure you make the most of your investment.

Chapter 7. Mastering the Art of Property Management

Before delving into the intricacies of mastering property management, it's important to understand its cornerstone - property management is the operation, control, and oversight of real estate. A skilled property manager will potentially enhance the value of your investment, thus, enabling you to build a solid foundation for your budding real estate empire. The promise of financial freedom lies essentially upon your ability to harness and exercise the various elements involved in managing properties effectively.

7.1. The Basics of Property Management

Let's start by understanding the need for property management. Purchasing an investment property is merely the first step towards developing a real estate portfolio. Managing that property is an ongoing process that demands continuous attention. Acquiring property might seem like a significant triumph - admittedly, it is - but what follows is an equally challenging task: preserving and enhancing the value of your property.

Your primary responsibilities as a property manager can be neatly categorised under four headings:

1. Tenant management - This involves tenant screening, rental collect, dispute resolution and eviction procedures if required.

2. Maintenance and repairs - This means ensuring the property stays in optimal condition which includes routine repairs, preventative maintenance, and extensive repairs or improvements.

3. Budgeting and financial management - This accounts for managing the property's financials, including budgeting for improvements, maintaining records, and generating income and expense reports.

4. Legal matters - Take care of all legal aspects, from local laws to fair housing regulations.

7.2. Conquering Tenant Management

A significant fraction of property management involves managing tenants effectively. This encompasses finding creditworthy tenants, drafting comprehensive lease agreements, collecting rents on time, handling tenant concerns, and diplomatically dealing with eviction if necessary.

7.2.1. Screening Tenants

Screening tenants is the first line of defence against potential difficulties that may arise during the lease period. Your screening process should be expressly designed to yield the most compatible tenant for your property, considering factors such as credit score, employment status, past rental history and references.

7.2.2. Drafting Lease Agreements

A comprehensive lease agreement is your legal safeguard. It serves to outline the terms and conditions of the lease, including rent amount and due date, damage deposits, lease term, and tenant responsibilities.

7.2.3. Rental Collection

Timely rental collection is crucial to maintaining a consistent cash flow. As a property manager, you should consistently enforce rent collection policies and procedures to ensure that payments are received on time.

7.2.4. Handling Tenant Concerns

Maintain an open line of communication with your tenants to address their concerns promptly. Their feedback could be invaluable in maintaining and improving your property.

7.3. Understanding and Overseeing Maintenance and Repairs

With ownership or management of a property come the responsibilities of maintaining it. Maintenance and repair can be classified into two general types: routine or preventive and extensive or reactive.

7.3.1. Routine Maintenance

Routine maintenance includes everyday tasks, like cleaning communal spaces, caretaking of green spaces, cautioning about potential issues, and conducting regular inspections.

7.3.2. Extensive Repairs

After several years, every property will require significant repairs or improvements. Whether this involves refurbishing the porch or replacing the roof, necessary preparations and budget allocations are crucial.

7.4. Mastering Budgeting and Financial Management

Accurate financial recordkeeping and budgeting are the heart of successful property management. Creating a realistic budget means evaluating income against expenses, considering factors like mortgage payments, insurance, taxes, maintenance, and potential vacancies.

7.4.1. Financial Record Keeping

Keep detailed records of all income and expenditures related to the property. This includes everything from rental payments, cost of repairs and maintenance, to insurance premiums and tax payments.

7.4.2. Budgeting

Track your expenses and income to create a comprehensive and effective budget. Use this budget to scrutinize your income versus your expenses and make projections about your property's potential profitability.

7.5. Navigating Through Legal Matters

Understanding the law will safeguard you and your property from potential legal disputes. You need to be well-versed with the Federal Fair Housing Act, which prohibits discrimination by landlords. Additionally, the laws regarding safety regulations, eviction procedures and landlord-tenant laws differ from state to state, thus a solid awareness is necessary.

7.5.1. Federal Fair Housing Act

This prohibits discrimination against tenants based on race, color, national origin, religion, sex, familial status or disability. Violations of the Act could lead to hefty fines.

7.5.2. State and Local Laws

While federal laws apply across the country, property management is also governed by state and local laws. These laws may deal with rent control, safety regulations, and eviction rules. It's crucial to familiarize yourself with these legal aspects to avoid breaches.

Successfully mastering the art of property management can seem daunting, but with this thorough guide, you are equipped with the necessary tools to navigate through even the most challenging scenarios. Don't be daunted by the work ahead. Every great empire was built one brick at a time - your property portfolio will be no different.

Chapter 8. Risk Management in Real Estate: Protecting your Investments

Real estate investment, while often lucrative, also carries inherent risks. The key to successfully navigating the unpredictable waters of property investment lies not in avoiding risks, but in understanding and managing them effectively. By integrating efficient risk management strategies into your investment portfolio, you can safeguard your investments against potential downturns, mitigating losses and enhancing your prospects for long-term growth.

8.1. Identifying Risks

Before you can manage risks, you must first learn to identify them accurately. Real estate investment risks can generally be categorized into market risks, asset-level risks, credit risks, and operational risks.

Market Risks pertain to fluctuations in market fundamentals, including changes in interest rates, inflation, and general economic conditions that can affect property valuations and rental income.

Asset-Level Risks relate to factors inherent to the specific property, such neighborhood demographics, physical condition of the property, and potential for natural disasters.

Credit Risks involve the likelihood of borrowers defaulting on their loans, impacting both individual lenders and the larger financial market.

Operational Risks are associated with the day-to-day management of real estate undertakings and can include regulatory changes, legal disputes, and management failures.

Investors must regularly conduct comprehensive market research and due diligence processes to identify and evaluate these various potential risks.

8.2. Developing a Risk Management Strategy

In developing your risk management strategy, the primary goal is to minimize the potential of financial loss. This involves several key steps:

1. **Risk Assessment**: Identify and categorize risks, quantifying them where possible to understand their potential impact on your investment.

2. **Risk Response**: Each identified risk will necessitate a strategy - you may choose to accept, transfer, mitigate, or avoid the risk entirely.

3. **Contingency Planning**: Design a plan of action tailored to each potential risk. This plan should seek to minimize the likelihood of the risk occurring, or diminish the impact should it transpire.

It's imperative to consider potential risks in both the short and long term. A property may present significant short-term profits while carrying long-term risks that could adversely affect your profitability.

8.3. Risk Diversification

Perhaps the most classic risk management strategy is diversification, or the practice of spreading investments across various types of assets. In the real estate context, this might mean investing in different types of properties (e.g. commercial, residential, industrial etc.) in varied locations, ensuring that a downturn in one sector or region doesn't wholly impact your investment portfolio.

Choosing a range of investments isn't just about spreading risk, however. A successful diversification strategy also seeks to capitalize on the advantages of each type of property, leveraging differences in risk and return to maximize overall profitability.

8.4. Insurance and Risk Transfer

Insurance plays a crucial role in risk management. By transferring potential financial consequences of certain risks to an insurance company, you can significantly mitigate financial loss.

Property insurance can cover a variety of risks, from physical damage to rental income losses resulting from untenantable conditions. Liability insurance is also vital to protect against the possibility of lawsuits from third parties.

For larger portfolios, investor may consider diversified insurance portfolios that spread the risk across different insurers.

8.5. Reserves and Liquidity

Maintaining ample liquid reserves is another fundamental risk management strategy. A cash reserve set aside for maintenance, repairs, vacancies, and unforeseen circumstances can prevent a precarious financial situation from turning into a full-blown crisis.

Remaining liquid also gives an investor flexibility to seize new investment opportunities as they arise and cover any downturns in rental income.

8.6. Legal and Regulatory Compliance

Legal and regulatory risks are other major considerations in real estate investing. These typically relate to zoning laws, tenant rights, and building code requirements.

Active monitoring of regulation changes, proactive compliance measures, and a solid understanding of the law is essential to ensure the long-term stability and legality of your property investments.

In conclusion, risk management is not a one-time event, but a continuous process of vigilance and adaptation. By integrating effective risk management into your real estate investment strategy, you can protect your assets, ensuring they continue to be a wealth-generating powerhouse for years to come.

Chapter 9. The Role of Diversification in Real Estate Empire-Building

In real estate, as in the broader world of investment, diversification is a critical strategy for risk management. One might consider it the finance equivalent of the ancient adage "don't put all your eggs in one basket." By spreading investments across a variety of properties and market segments, individuals can shield their portfolios from potential downturns in a single area. But diversification within the realm of real estate investment extends beyond the concept of variety. It involves exploiting differences in market dynamics, local economies, and property types—all while striking a balance between risk and reward.

9.1. Understanding Diversification

In the field of finance, diversification refers to the method of allocating capital in a manner that mitigates risk by investing in a variety of assets. If one asset performs poorly, others might perform well and counterbalance the loss. To achieve such balance in real estate, investors may diversify in multiple ways: by property type, geography, investment size, industry, and property use, to name a few.

The principles of diversification hold true whether you're investing in real estate directly—buying land or property—or indirectly through Real Estate Investment Trusts (REITs) or real estate crowdfunding platforms. Primary examples of property diversification could include spreading your portfolio among residential, commercial, retail, and industrial properties.

9.2. Diversification by Property Type

Different types of properties tend to react differently to varied economic situations. A prime example is the comparison between commercial properties – which can be highly sensitive to economic cycles – and residential properties, which exhibit a higher degree of resilience, mostly due to the perpetual demand for housing. Thus, a diversified portfolio might include a mix of commercial and residential properties, thereby spreading the risk.

Within the residential sector itself, investors could consider diversifying across single-family homes, multi-family units, condos, and townhouses. Each comes with its own set of dynamics and benefits. For example, multi-family unit properties may generate a more steady income, since the vacancy of a single unit doesn't render the whole property unproductive. Similarly, within the commercial segment, a variety of offices, retail spaces, and industrial properties are available for exploration.

9.3. Diversification by Geography

Geographical diversification is another vital component, enabling investors to tap into different local economies and real estate markets. The real estate valuation and rental yield profiles in New York, Chicago, or Houston, for example, would differ significantly from smaller towns in the Midwest or coastal suburbs in Florida. International diversification also garners traction among investors aspiring to exploit international growth trends and currency dynamics.

As with most investments, the rewards usually come with risks. Expanding your real estate investments to new locations might expose you to unfamiliar market dynamics and regulatory environments. Therefore, adequate research and consultation with local market experts could be the precursor to beneficial geographical diversification.

9.4. Diversification by Investment Size

Diversification can also be achieved at different investment scales. While large, multi-million dollar commercial projects could offer substantial returns, they also require more capital and often bring added complexity and risk. Alternatively, investing in smaller assets such as single-family homes or smaller multi-unit complexes, investors can start earning returns sooner and with less upfront costs. A diverse portfolio could include both small and large-scale investments, aligning with the investor's budget, risk tolerance, and wealth-building objectives.

9.5. Diversification through REITs and Crowdfunding Platforms

For investors who prefer a more indirect approach to real estate investment, diversification can be achieved through investment in Real Estate Investment Trusts (REITs) or crowdfunding platforms. These options can offer a broad exposure to various kinds of real estate investments with a lesser amount of capital compared to direct property ownership. Furthermore, these investment pools are managed by professionals, saving investors the hassle of property management.

However, as convenient as these indirect routes are, they come with their own sets of risks. An investor might not fully understand what is in the pool of properties that a REIT or crowdfunding platform invests in, and liquidity may also be an issue. Therefore, risk assessment and due diligence become vital for successful diversification through these indirect channels.

9.6. Balancing Risk and Reward through Diversification

Successful real estate diversification strikes the correct balance between risk and reward, and such balance differs from one investor to another. Risk tolerance is largely subjective and may be influenced by factors like age, income level, long-term financial goals, and overall investment experience. Therefore, while diversification is intended to spread and mitigate risk, it's crucial to align diversification strategies with individual risk tolerance levels.

There may also be times when concentration, rather than diversification, is a more effective strategy for certain investors. For instance, focusing on a specific sub-sector like student housing or assisted living facilities, particularly when the investor is well-versed in these areas, could yield more profitable outcomes. Therefore, while diversification plays a significant role in managing risk, it should be exercised sensibly and strategically.

Becoming a successful real estate investor involves acquiring an in-depth understanding of market dynamics, meticulous planning, and execution, as well as portfolio diversification. The intricate process of diversification calls for expertise in different property types, regions, and investment sizes. By understanding and applying effective diversification strategies, investors stand a better chance at building a resilient real estate empire – one that can withstand economic uncertainties and continuously provide stable returns.

Chapter 10. Selling and Expanding: Your Guide to Growth

One aspect that separates the casual player from the master in real estate is the winning approach towards property sale, expansion, and growth. Sustained success requires more than merely buying low and selling high; instead, it demands a carefully crafted strategy, forethought, and diligent execution. In this chapter, we delve deeply into the art of property selling and expansion, offering you a winning guide to sustainable growth.

10.1. The Art of Selling

Selling property is a delicate dance between timing, pricing, negotiation, and market conditions. While some investors believe that any sale that brings profit is good, the real connoisseurs understand that maximizing this profit is vital.

1. **Timing the sale:** Just like buying, timing your sale is crucial. It's not just about market conditions but also about the seasonality of the real estate market in your area. For instance, residential properties often sell better in late spring and early autumn. On the other hand, commercial properties aren't as impacted by seasons but depend more on economic cycles.

2. **Pricing your property:** While it may seem like a good idea to set a high price and then negotiate down, in reality, overpriced properties can scare away potential buyers. A more effective strategy is to price your property competitively, attracting multiple interested buyers and possibly initiating a bidding war.

3. **Marketing and advertising:** Employing an effective marketing strategy can do wonders for your sale. This can range from

professional photos and virtual tours to hosting open houses. Leveraging the power of social media can also expose your property to a wider audience.

10.2. Expansion: Feeding Your Growth

After securing profits from your sales, the next step is to reinvest those profits into new properties, further fuelling your empire's growth. This process is nuanced, and careful consideration should be taken in choosing where to invest next.

1. **Market research:** Understanding where to invest next necessitates a deep understanding of real estate market trends, from neighborhood revitalizations to shifts in economic policies that could influence property values.

2. **Evaluating properties:** Once you've selected a potential property, a thorough property evaluation is crucial. This includes studying the property's condition, site location, potential rental income and even potential emergency repairs.

3. **Risk management and diversification:** To mitigate the potential risks involved in real estate investment, it's important to diversify your investments. This can be achieved through different property types (residential, commercial, industrial) or even venturing into different locations/marketplaces.

10.3. Financing Your Expansion

To continuously grow your real estate empire, you'll need to focus not only on what properties to acquire but also how to fund these acquisitions. Mastering the financing methods available can transform your real estate venture from a passive income hobby into a booming empire.

1. **Mortgages:** Leveraging mortgages is a common way to finance new acquisitions, enabling you to purchase properties that might be otherwise out of reach.

2. **Hard money loans:** These are usually short-term, high-interest loans that are commonly used for flipping properties.

3. **Private money lenders:** These could be anyone from family and friends to business connections who lend you money for your investments.

4. **Partnerships or syndications:** Teaming up with others can make pricier property purchases possible, often providing access to larger and potentially more lucrative deals.

Proper expansion in real estate is a well-balanced mix of selling properties strategically, investing in new ones thoughtfully, and managing your finances effectively. Understanding these crucial concepts and exhibiting patience and persistence can lead to sustained success, allowing you to truly build your empire through property.

Chapter 11. Sustaining Wealth: The Long-term Perspective of Property Investment

The cornerstone of sustained wealth from property investment is a sound long-term strategy. Whether you're banking on consistent rental income or anticipating future capital appreciation, understanding the key components of successful long-term investing is vital. Let's delve into these components and how they contribute to sustained wealth creation.

11.1. Understanding Market Cycles

The real estate market moves in cycles, just like any other marketplace. It has periods of boom, bust, recovery, and stability. These cycles are influenced by various external factors like the economy, demand and supply dynamics, interest rates, and government policies. Here is a brief overview of the four phases:

1. Recovery: Characterized by low demand, stagnant property prices, and a surplus of unsold properties.

2. Growth: High demand leads to a surge in property prices. The market becomes a seller's market.

3. Peak: Property prices hit a maximum before demand stagnates or starts tapering.

4. Decline: Demand for properties decreases, leading to a correction in property prices.

Understanding these cycles can help you make better-informed decisions about when to buy, hold, or sell properties. Remember, the goal is not to try and time the market but to comprehend and navigate these cycles effectively.

11.2. Investing in Prime Locations

Location plays a pivotal role in property investment. It determines the kind of return on investment (ROI) you can expect and how your investment will perform in the long term. When deciding on a location, consider factors like proximity to amenities, growth potential, market saturation, etc.

Prime locations tend to command higher rentals and show consistent capital appreciation. They are vibrant with commercial and social infrastructure, making them desirable for renters and buyers alike. Additionally, properties in prime locations tend to recover faster from market downturns.

11.3. Diversifying Your Portfolio

Like any investment venture, diversification is critical in property investment. Diversification can take several forms - by property type (residential, commercial, industrial), by geography (local, regional, international), or even by investment strategy (buy-to-let, fix-and-flip, REITs).

The key objective behind diversifying your property portfolio is to spread the risks. It ensures that a setback in one property or market doesn't significantly affect the whole portfolio.

11.4. Improving Cash Flow Management

A prime strategy for sustaining long-term wealth through property investment lies in improved cash flow management. Positive cash flows can be obtained through rental income, which must surpass your mortgage repayments, maintenance costs, taxes, and other expenses.

Investors need to consider their fixed (like mortgage payments and property taxes) and variable costs (such as maintenance and vacancy periods) when computing their cash flows. Regularly reviewing your cash flow and making necessary adjustments is vital for the long-term sustainability of your investments.

11.5. The Power of Leverage

Leverage refers to the use of borrowed funds for investment, with the property itself serving as collateral. In property investment, leverage allows you to buy properties that you may not be able to afford upfront.

While leveraging increases your potential for profit, it also amplifies the risk. Therefore, proper risk assessment and management are crucial when using leverage. Sensible leveraging can maximize your returns and potentially expedite your wealth generation.

11.6. Managing Risks in Property Investment

Risk management is another key aspect of sustainable property investment. This includes identifying, assessing, and mitigating risks. Some common risks in property investment include:

1. Market Risk: The risk of property values going down due to market dynamics.
2. Liquidity Risk: Difficulty in selling the property when needed.
3. Credit Risk: The risk of default from tenants leading to loss of rental income.

4. Damage and Repair Risk: The risk of damage to the property leading to decrease in property's value and unexpected repair costs.

Risk management strategies may include diversifying the portfolio, having an emergency fund, obtaining suitable insurance, robust tenant screening, and regular property maintenance.

11.7. The Importance of Patience

Property investing is often depicted as a get-rich-quick scheme. However, it requires a degree of patience and persistence. Sustaining wealth through property investment is not about making one lucrative deal but about continually growing and managing your portfolio over the years.

Stay patient and stay the course, focusing on long-term wealth creation over short-term gains.

In conclusion, the long-term perspective to property investment entails a keen understanding of market cycles, identifying key locations, portfolio diversification, robust cash flow management, sensible use of leverage, effective risk management and, above all, patience. By applying these strategies effectively, you can sustain and grow wealth from your property investments over the long term.